CHICKENSH!T

CHICKENSH!T

DeAnna Durant

© Copyright 2019 DeAnna Durant

All rights reserved. No part of this book may be used or reproduced in any manner whatsoever without written permission of the author except in the case of brief quotations embodied in critical articles and reviews.

The information in this book is distributed as an "as is" basis, without warranty. Although, every precaution has been taken in the preparation of this work, neither the author or the publisher shall have any liability to any person or entity with respect to any loss or damage caused or alleged to be caused directly or indirectly by the information contained in this book.

The content is not intended to be substituted for professional medical advice, diagnosis, or treatment. Always seek the advice of your physician or other qualified health provider with any questions you may have regarding a medical condition. Never disregard professional medical advice or delay in seeking it because of something you have read in this book.

Printed in the United States of America.
ISBN: 979-8-89170-092-5
Cover Design & Interior Book Design: DeAnna Durant

DEDICATION

A thousand thanks to my hero Gary and my dear friend Nancy, for being there for me through my most difficult times.
Gary, I can't count how many people you've been there for! I am grateful for all you've done for me.

To Candis, Johnny, Trayce, Phyllis, Jeff and my friend Greg for lending an ear to listen, a shoulder to cry on and a hand to hold.

And to Vinci, my heart & soul, who has taught me so much and who I am so proud of.

To my mother Linda & daddy John
and my daddy Gary. I wish I had more time with each of you, and my grandparents.

My deepest heartfelt thanks,
for your guidance, love & laughter, and your presence, I am eternally grateful that I was lucky enough to be born into my family and to know so many beautiful hearts.
God Bless You.

"Shit or get off the pot."

> A military colloquialism

Table of Contents

	Preface	1
1	Cock-a-doodle-doo!	3
2	Henpeck	33
3	Hard-Boiled	53
4	Chickensh!t	75
5	Chicken Scratch	99
	Dear Reader,	135
	The Brood	137

CHICKENSH!T

PREFACE

We get sick & tired of it, and take it all the time, yet can't take it anymore! Most of us don't give it, and others give it too much! We've been served a bunch, a pile, a heap , a crock of it, and our fair share of it!

Others die from eating it, dip it and have it for brains! Where some people can be a piece of it, and completely full of it!

We've sat in it, stepped in it, scooped it, put it on shingles, talked it, dealt it, smelt it, cut it, stress on it, been knee deep in it and had it up to here from dealing with it. It's even hit the fan! That usually happens when someone doesn't think theirs stinks.
We still don't know it from Shinola.
Do we even know what Shinola is?

Whether we blame our pucky on the bull, a horse, a dog, or the chicken, it's an inevitable mess. An uncontrollable force of nature and we are never going to stop it!

We've tried to polish it and at the very least cover its scent. It can run fast, but only takes second place! The famous number 2, the deuce!

CHICKENSH!T

If it's not coming out the end it's supposed to, then it is the other, and that's when it gets hard to put up with! It's the heat packing a loose cannon that has everyone walking on eggshells!

If it's because they're plugged up, backed up, or jacked up, nobody should have to feel like they are up to their ears in it! The good news is, that it is manageable with a balanced diet and a good laxative!

If you've been suffering from these fecal matters, then this pocketbook of poopy chickiblical proverbs may be the suppository you've been looking for!

If this doesn't give one the urge to get theirs together instead of making it harder for those helping to wipe up their mess, you might have to get an entire fleet of peeps involved. We can all use a fresh start from time to time!

May this be the plop-plop, fizz-fizz that offers you the relief from what binds you without having to drink something that tastes like what you need the relief from!

I hope this can assist in your smooth move forward, to flush it all away, and leave the worst, behind, because none of us have time for it!

Unless you're the Tidy Bowl man!

1

Cock-a-doodle-doo!
Wake Up Call!

Most of us have heard the rhyme, "Sticks and stones may break my bones, but words will never hurt me." It's been a classis retort for verbally bullied children for generations. If a bully's goal is to hurt someone, then it implies that words will fail, and physical violence will succeed. Even if the response is said to dissolve a physical quarrel, and that words cannot harm us the way coming to blows can.

No matter our age, the longer we are verbally abused the more debilitating it becomes. Words are powerful enough to break hearts, spirits, and people apart.

Sure, there are endless reasons a person resorts to boorish or bad behavior, but "two wrongs don't make it right", and what may be considered a phase can become a lifelong habit if we let it.

Everyone is capable of bad behavior. It's when it's ingrained that it becomes a toxic. Toxic traits are not exclusive to clinical disorders; anybody can bear them; self-included. The idea is to control our behavior before it controls us.

Just as easily as a bad habit can form, so can a good habit; like being more conscientious with our words and actions.

Some habits are harder to break than a heart, but the good news is that habits can be broken, and hearts can heal.

There will be moments that we hurt other people whether we intend to or not, and it's nice to receive reminders or an unexpected wake-up call from time to time.

Thank goodness for the good ol' rooster summoning the sun so that we can all see the light.

The bird really is the word!

CHICKENSH!T

Some people will tell you:
How to be, instead of asking how you are.
What to think, instead of asking what you think.
How to feel, instead of asking how you feel.

They demand respect from people they haven't any for.

Questions like "How are you?" or "Whatcha doing?" Are considered prying, instead of meaning well.

There are the doers, and there are the people that like to sit on their ass telling the doers what to do. No! This isn't their parent, teacher, boss, or anybody they work for; these are the people that DON'T. They either want to discourage the doers or tell the doers how to do it!

CHICKENSH!T

They expect from others, what they are fully capable of doing themself.

Adults that didn't learn from their parents' discipline as children, usually have no self-discipline as adults.

Their exes always want them back.

You might not know right away how devious they are, but their friends will, and they don't usually have them long.

You can run around like a chicken with its head cut off, and it's never enough.

They lack the self-discipline that most seven-year-olds have mastered!

They must have been miserable to shit on someone that cared.

You will never win the heart of an intelligent person by talking to them like they're a child.

Treat others as you wish to be treated. It's the Golden Rule. Never forget it!

They'll know how hard it is to do something for themself and will disrespect the people helping them do it.

You will need mental help because they won't get it.

They break things if they don't get their way.

CHICKENSH!T

A person that won't listen to constructive criticism will stunt their emotional growth and think they are the wiser, while everyone around them is growing up.

Do you remember the rule from the previous page? Try before you check.

Did you remember?

They are in the habit of saying they'll do it later, then forget to do it at all.

CHICKENSH!T

They behave as if they are the only one to work hard. If they work at all.

An adult that expects others to clean up their messes is like saying, who needs potty training if someone else will wipe my ass.

If you're called a dog, then take it as a compliment, dogs are honorable and loving and deserve to have people pick up their shit.

Toxic people are very good about making you feel bad for doing good things for them.

They don't take advice, they take advantage.

If it wasn't their intention to make you cry, then they would console you.

They screech louder than Yoko Ono and think strength is a word found on a hat or t-shirt!

They claim it is impossible, while watching you do it.

You've watched small children disciplined for less.

They believe the opinions of others are about them. Everything it's all about them!

They won't contribute to rent, or the essential bills being paid, and they bitch about how hard they have it.

CHICKENSH!T

They put words in other people's mouths because they lack credibility. "So and so said..."

Losers really do lose things.
Wallets, jobs, partners, friends, keys.
Not just occasionally. ALL the time and usually because they lose their temper!

They hate you for being a good person, but still want good things from you.

People that talk bad about people behind their back, are giving those people a reason to talk about them behind theirs.

CHICKENSH!T

If anything goes wrong for a coward, those around them will suffer the consequences.

Jive is for turkeys.

BTW, being a coward is not limited to a male.

They'll have you doubting and second guessing yourself.

Memories aren't supposed to be reminders of all the times they hurt you.

Don't kid yourself! A stay at home mom has a job.

Shit fire and save the matches.

If you've witnessed what their bad vibes can do, just imagine what they'd accomplish with positive vibes.

If you did to them what they do to you, they would throw a massive tantrum.

Being bored is an excuse to have something to bitch about. There are plenty of things to do.

They accuse you of thinking something that they think, then hold you accountable for their thought.

CHICKENSH!T

They not only make problems worse than they are, but they also make it harder for you to take care of the problem for them.

They think of who can improve their situation before they consider how they can.

They use you into needing the help of other people too.

They are the first to squawk over anything challenging.

CHICKENSH!T

If an abuser hears people, it inspires them. <- FACTS!

A toxic person will try and destroy every positive thing you do, and sometimes the positive things you do for them.

Amends is the difference between a mistake and doing something deliberate.

Most people listen to understand, they listen to respond and judge.

If you are hurt, then they are hurt more.

Invites are lures If they want something from you.

If you were a loser, you wouldn't have read this far.

Seeing good people enjoying themselves pisses them off.

You can bend over backwards for them and if you need a simple favor, they will have an excuse for why they can't, they delay doing it, or forget about it altogether.

They will suck the life out of your beautiful soul, then claim they loved you the most.

If you recognize when you need to apologize and feel bad . Then you have something no amount of money can buy.

CHICKENSH!T

Be careful when a person tells you someone isn't good for you, that they aren't just as bad for you.

You will do just about anything to keep the peace.

They will turn the story around to their benefit.

They never hear the tone of their own voice.

A chickenshit, is mean, moody, and unwilling to challenge themselves to be better.

CHICKENSH!T

Doing something positive with your life concerns them, because, they have nothing better to do.

They try to put the kibosh on all your plans.

Oh! For crying out loud! Don't be such a party pooper!

Make sure what they came to you about is resolved before you bring up your issue or choose another time.

They stomp, talk under their breath, and slam things down demanding attention.

If you aren't praising them, then they are using their know-it-all mentality to draw attention to themselves.

They belittle you.

If it belongs to them, you return it better than before you used it. If it is yours, they don't put it back, they break it, or lose it, then claim they never touched it.

They will ask you for a place to stay, then do something to jeopardize the roof over your head.

They make you too uncomfortable to ask why they're being disrespectful.

CHICKENSH!T

The reason they have respect for authority is because it can make life harder for them, not because it will make life easier for everyone.

L-L-Listening, is n-n-not a r-r-reason t-to st-st-stutter! It's amazing how they can say, "I know!" 3 times fast without stuttering.

The, "Nobody tells me what to do!" mentality, usually ends up in a place where people must tell them what to do.

The people that think nobody can hear what they're saying when they whisper are the same people that think nobody will find out.

CHICKENSH!T

A cockerel struts around thinking he rules the roost!

They have their own rules you must abide, and the regular ones don't apply them.

A lot of people have court orders that allow a responsible person to manage their money because they won't.
Let this be initiative.

It is always about them!
Not "you" or "ours".
It is "theirs".
Their time, their feelings, their home, their day off.

If you stick your neck out, they'll chop your head off.

Quit squabbling over every little thing!

They leave messes for you to clean up or ultimately have to be asked to clean up their mess.

They limit your connections because they're afraid you'll confide in someone that might tell you how plucked up they are.

They use drama and tension to lord over the household.

Bullies belittle and humiliate you, lovers, and friends won't
.

CHICKENSH!T

They tell you that arguing is normal. It's NOT normal to argue about why they belittle and humiliate you all the time.

They talk under their breath.

The Golden Rule: Treat others as you wish to be treated.

Just because you treat others how you want to be treated, doesn't mean that other people will treat you as you have them. Be kind anyway.

CHICKENSH!T

A sounding board is not someone to scream at unless it's really a board but why would you do that.

A weak mentality has no idea the strength it takes for those around them to put up with them.

Home is where you should feel safe and protected, and where your heart is supposed to be. Unless a tyrant runs the household.

They make you regret being a nice person.

People that treat you like a child for having a difficult time, usually have other people doing everything for them.

If they wanted to resolve your relationship issues, they would quit talking about you, and talk to you!

Being around an angry person that is always ranting is incredibly debilitating, especially if they are an adult.

They push your buttons until they get a reaction, then use it to justify their behavior, instead of putting that much energy into not being overbearing.

They'll make a funeral about themself.

Their tension is one of your worst enemies, and theirs.

2

Henpeck
Frazzled Feathers

A "henpeck" is a derogatory term describing a nagging female who criticizes what other people do. The truth is, just because a henpeck is a female, it doesn't mean the behavior is limited to one.

Just like some people are known to twist situations around to their benefit, words can be twisted as well.

The term has been applied to people that have asked someone to do something important more than once. By suggesting that the person reminding them is the problem, they avoid accountability. Not to be confused with the actual definition of a henpeck.

Those who use this method to escape a responsibility often end up in a position where they rely on the same person they referred to as a henpeck, to help them.

CHICKENSH!T

Odds are, those that use it as an insult, bear the traits attributed to a henpeck. They are usually people with low self-esteem that like to push people's buttons until they get a reaction.

They might use a domineering chicken style pecking order to achieve rank amongst their siblings, peers, or household. This manipulation tactic can be carried from grade school to adulthood.

Those around them try to subdue their behavior which doesn't merit them any actual respect.

They tend to overreact to most everything; a sudden noise, something dropping, laughter or animal sounds. When there is a sound that would elicit a "gasp"; a loud boom, bang or crash, and the person that overreacts to everything else, would be the first to say something about how the person that gasped overreacted.

From petty ways to get attention that make us laugh more than anything, to outright emotional abuse that can suck the life and soul out of those subjected to it. They keep picking straws until they reach the one that breaks the camel's back. It can become so maddening we could spit feathers! That is their point, and it leaves us feeling frazzled.

They mistake kindness for stupidity.

They think that other people who look at them are staring and thinking something bad.

They cut you off or walk out when you are talking.

You will know when it is time to end a relationship long before you manage to, and that is when you will go through the worst.

Their rotten choices are always your phucken fault!

CHICKENSH!T

If you don't react when they want your attention, they will up the drama until they get it.

It's heart-wrenching when you're helping someone you love, and they blame you for being the reason they need help.

They do it so often that you begin to wonder if they contemplate making poor choices, just to hold other people accountable for them?

They will stifle you so bad that your cheeks and lips quiver.

CHICKENSH!T

They are condescending.

When you leave a toxic relationship, your abuser will blame god, because well, you know, they had nothing to do with it.

Strange how they blame you for everything but won't stay the pluck away from you.

Most people that point a finger to blame others, rely on them not to pull it. They don't because they know they are full of hot air, and we all know what proceeds that!

They rush to condemn someone else for less an offense than what they do on a regular basis.

An indication that a manipulative person is in control of those around them is that nobody else has a voice or an opinion of their own . If they try, and argument ensues.

They will betray you, then get pissed-off because you don't trust them!

A toxic person might use all the clinical terms to insult you, that apply to them, but you won't use them to abuse them because you know they have a problem.

CHICKENSH!T

Instead of considering why you have distanced yourself, they'll accuse you of ghosting them, which is probably what they did to you before you distanced yourself.

The reason they accuse you of doing so many things that you would never do, is because they are afraid that you are doing what they do to you that you don't know about.

Similarly, they know they can't be trusted, so they assume you can't be either.

They are only proud if it makes them look good.

CHICKENSH!T

Liars don't realize how easy it is for others to spot them. Most people never call them on it and the ones that do, they don't believe.

You think they have a disorder they can't control, until they conveniently change their attitude the moment someone unexpected shows up.

Wouldn't it be neat if this was the first time you read a whole book.

What can be nipped in the bud is blown completely out of proportion. "Mountains out of mole hills."

A toxic partner who claims to love you can easily throw you away, and when they want you to come back, they will ask why YOU gave up on them.

Don't worry if a lot of this shit applies to you, you're not alone and people have no choice but to grow.

If they apologize at all, their voice and demeanor are more disrespectful than what they did that required an apology to begin with.

Quit belittling everyone! Your partner, children, friends, co-workers, employees your boss and yourself; It's amazing how much a person can accomplish when they feel respect and appreciation.

If you're not sincere when you apologize, then you're not sorry.

They refer to your pain as anger.

CHICKENSH!T

If they are jealous, they don't have much to say.

No! They don't have the runs.
They're texting their ex!

Trivial things trigger them.

They browbeat you to get their way.

They bock about everybody behind their back.

CHICKENSH!T

If you're going to do something nice for someone, then why complain about doing it. It takes the "nice" part away and turns the opportunity into making a person feel like a burden. That's not nice.

They're always whining.

They do something they would never want done to them, and when you don't react, they'll ask you what's wrong, and when you answer, they say you just want to argue.

They conveniently schedule their meltdowns around the rare occasions that celebrate you.

They would rather get mad at you for not reading their mind than to tell you what it is on it.

They think you can read their mind because they think that they can read yours.

They are jealous of your accomplishments. No matter how great or small.

Moms really do have eyes in the back of their heads and experience is how it is achieved.

They think you're a henpeck because you reminded them about something important "Uh uh uh I'll get to it when I can!" Then they never get to it. And that'll probably be your fault too.

They brag about how smart they are but can't figure out why you would respond with the same sh!tty tone of voice they use when they talk to you?

CHICKENSH!T

They cry crocodile tears.

They have delusions of grandeur.

They will never let anybody live down what they are forgiven for all the time.

Don't just grow old, grow up, but stay young at heart.

They make plans for you and expect you to follow through.

CHICKENSH!T

You want to ease their stress and they prefer to stress you out so that you will do what it takes to ease theirs.

They put words into your mouth that you've never said.

The tone of voice they use when apologizing can tell you if they are sincere or not. Sometimes the apology makes you feel worse than the offense they are apologizing for.

They humiliate you in front of other people and because of it, are unaware they embarrass themselves more.

They patronize you.

They credit themselves with anything successful you do.

They are almost always bored.

When they think your opinion of them has changed, and that you are confiding in others about it, this is when they will start talking bad about you to the same people, they use to fawn over you with.

They are incredibly immature.

They prefer tantrums over strength.

3

Hard-Boiled
What the pluck?

We all have times of trouble and need someone we can go to for emotional support or to help bail us out of a desperate situation.

It has been said that when you do something nice for another person, to not expect anything in return. It should also be said, that if you don't show appreciation for the people who have been there, then they might not consider being there again. (Agreements and negotiations should always be honored.)

Nobody expects a 'paragon of virtue', but it's in our favor to be honorable and remain in good standing with people willing to be there in a pinch. Those are our peeps! They care!

CHICKENSH!T

The environment we grow up in helps to shape our outlook on life, love, and responsibility. Home should be the safest place a person can be and if it's full of tension, not keeping promises and arguing instead of security and love, then we can attain a more cynical way of looking at life and the world.

Values become ways to try and shock people rather than something to cherish. And making memories is more comparable to "what the pluck" moments, that we have a hard enough time trying to wrap our head around, let alone explain.

Combined all this together and you'll have all the earmarks of an emotionally defect, hard-boiled individual, with a suspicious mind. Always looking for clues to create a case for something not happening. Ask Elvis, you just can go on, or build dreams with a mind like that.

I hope the following random examples help to make conveying your own experiences a little easier to crack.

It's been said that if you want to know how you'll be treated in a relationship, then look to how your partners' parents treat one another. More importantly, how does your partner treat their parents?

If they apologize, and I stress "IF", they either won't know what they are apologizing for, or they won't know which time to address, if they remember any at all.

They feel reprimanded if you question why they hurt you.

Quit mistaking "Karma" for your own heart delighting in the hardship of someone you don't like.

If a parent teaches their child to disrespect the custodial parent, then the child won't have any parents.

Teaching a child to disrespect their other parent takes the joy of being a parent away, it makes being able to parent difficult and cheats everyone out of happiness, especially the child.

Lose a rude-tude.

CHICKENSH!T

Don't discuss your adult issues with your child. They are not your parent.

A child is not an object to use against the other parent.

Young hearts and brains are molded by example, set a good one.

They say things like, "you need help" to insult you, instead of helping you.

CHICKENSH!T

How parents regard one another in front of their child, whether they are together or not, is usually how they will treat their partner when they grow up. Don't set them up for failure.

A mother provides life support to her baby before its born and after, until the child reaches 18. If they are taught not to listen to her, then they will have a difficult life.

Hearing you cry infuriates them.

They demand their rights be met when they are in another person's territory and strip the rights of those whose territory it is!

They are sneaky, and always suspicious of you.

They one-up you.

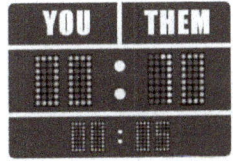

"What they don't know won't hurt them", is not always true.

Five basic things every mother teaches a child to know by age five.

1. Not to lie.
2. Ask before they borrow.
3. Put things back where they got them.
4. Clean up after themselves.
5. Be respectful.
6.

How old are you?

They didn't help make the bread but eat all of it before anybody else gets some.

It's a mad scramble when something ticks them off!

CHICKENSH!T

If you really needed help, why wouldn't they want to help you?

Quiet crying is one of the hardest things to do.

They stroke their ego at the expense of your heart.

If the abuse is damaging you that much, just imagine what it is doing to your children.

CHICKENSH!T

If you finally draw the line, they'll fall into a trance!

The truth doesn't hurt them because they believe a lie.

Whatever it is you think they think of you, it's because you have thought it of yourself.

If it didn't make them happy to stomp around making those around them uncomfortable, then they wouldn't do it.

They wouldn't be able to put up with themselves without a cockfight ensuing.

You were supposed to laugh.

The only person comfortable in an abusive relationship is the abuser. Not you, your kids, friends, family, or guests; they're all uncomfortable.

You don't owe anybody your soul, your honesty is enough. Keep your word.

You can disagree and not invalidate someone. Though, there are people that take offense no matter how kind you are about it.

Quit cutting people off mid-sentence when they remind you of certain responsabilities and consider what would happen if they didn't.

CHICKENSH!T

What is clinically known as "Narcissistic rage" makes a narcissist feel powerful. To other people it looks like, this doofus is way too old to be throwing a phucken tantrum.

You can be understand someone was hurt by something you did, without having intended to hurt them.

Bad choices affect more people than the person making them.

Stop being your child's worst influence.

CHICKENSH!T

Why are you so
PISSED OFF

If you mellowed out and appreciated what you have you'd learn to be happy instead of stealing everyone's peace. Take Lamaze if you have to.

If you're not a chickensh!t, then stop acting like you are.

They are always scheming, always hatching something.

They dangle carrots.

- Petty people
- Do petty things
- To create a petty issue
- To get your reaction
- Then they'll tell you how petty you are.

They use the excuse that they didn't want to get into trouble, when you find out they didn't tell you about something that could cause lots of trouble, and they are over 50 years old.
(That can be bad or sad)

They get angry when asked to do things that nobody should have to be asked to do.

"I know, I know!" They whine. As if they haven't given you plenty of reason to be concerned.
If they "knew", they wouldn't need your help!

Appreciate the people who help pay your consequences when you get into trouble. They don't have to help! How would you get to court, school, or to work project if it weren't for them?

People really do get physically sick from dealing with other people's shit.

CHICKENSH!T

They are more pissed off at the people helping them than the people that should be pissed off, are at them.

They never forgive you for the things they do!

They tell the person they are cheating with that YOU are a bad person. ... Birds of a feather, eh.

Weak characters are jealous of their partners. Strong one's uplift and encourage them.

CHICKENSH!T

They body shame you, then call you insecure.

If you don't participate in their argument, they will put words in your mouth based upon what they think you would say. Then believe you've said it.

They know the latest coop scoop.

They flip their wig! Don't wig out!

If caught betraying you, they suggest it was for your own good.

Someone else told them to do it.

"ITS ALL YOUR FAULT!

They make excuses for their behavior.

Insulting their intelligence makes you look stoopid. So don't do it.

When a child isn't nurtured about why it's wrong, they will grow up thinking it is normal.

They count their chickens before they hatch.

CHICKENSH!T

It's never too late to become the best version of you!

Entitlement starts with being concerned with who is going to get you what you want, or what it is going to take for them to get it for you, instead of thinking how you can get it yourself.

Similarly, some people grow up thinking they had it hard because their parent(s) had to work harder than most to get them the things they wanted.

"Do as I say not as I do", is a way of telling a child that when they grow up, they can set a bad example too.

CHICKENSH!T

Whatever lie they convince themselves they aren't telling, they think they've convinced others of.

They say, "Everybody knows I love you!" Who cares if everybody knows! You need to know and you're not even in their loop.

They are full of fauxpologies and sh!t.
Stand back!

4

Chickenshit
Fowl Behavior!

I remember my mother referring to a "chickenshit" as anybody driven by fear and insecurity that gets what they want at the expense of someone else. Along with a lack of conscience when it comes to how their actions can affect others, at the same time knowing exactly what they are doing. e.g., a cheap shot, wise cracks that makes someone the brunt of their joke, compromising safety for entertainment, passing the buck, public humiliation, accusing someone else of doing something they do all the time, expecting that person to get into trouble.

"The pot calling the kettle black". Always pointing out what they consider a flaw about someone else to cover a flaw of their own, without realizing that they draw attention to worse attributes than the one they are trying to hide, like hypocrisy.

If you confide in them, it goes in one ear and out their mouths and into the ears of every Tom, Dick, and Harry they know.

Chickenshit behavior is usually a choice and stops the moment the person chooses not to be. Sometimes facing our own darkness is frightening, but it's a courageous thing to do.

It is also important to consider that there are people that feel the need to pull things out of thin air and accuse someone for something they haven't done, just to feel better about themselves.

If someone that is genuinely hurt, they deserve their feelings acknowledged and a sincere apology is usually all it takes to remedy the issue.

This is not that easy! In fact, they might come to you with something that you haven't done, and because they've said you hurt them, you apologize, stating that there must be a misunderstanding and it was not your intention .

CHICKENSH!T

Only now, they accuse you of invalidating their feelings and it becomes a "damned if you do and damned if you don't" situation. It's genuine chickenshit!

They don't really want an apology from you, they want someone to argue with. It's not really about their feelings, it's about attacking yours.

When you decide to ask why they are affronting you, they deny it, which is referred to as, gaslighting. You might not even know what gaslighting is and are about to be given a firsthand lesson, when they accuse you of gaslighting them, as they are gaslighting you!

Read that twice if you must! If it made your head spin, that is exactly what gaslighting feels like. It's a mind game and its cruel.

All of us have done something chickenshit in our lives, and it may have been the pivotal moment that teaches us why we should never do it again!

Life is fleeting, and we deal with enough shit that comes naturally than to be creating more of it. No pun intended, "fleeting"! But yeah, if it takes an enema, so be it!

CHICKENSH!T

They're bagossips.

I promise! It stinks!

They are sanctimonious.

If we don't grow out of it, then we grow up and it grows out of control.

Some people prefer manipulation to breaking the habit.

An ornery adult will do something in front of their mother that she taught them not to do because it makes them feel more like an adult than respect does.

Normal doesn't mean you have to be perfect. It means you recognize what you need to work on make an effort to change it.

They don't consider that you may need to get help to help them.

They either take good care of their things or they don't. Either way, they don't care about your things.

Reiterating a rule can make it click.

They boast and are begrudging.

It's only human, the first time you do it. After you know better it's chickenshit!

CHICKENSH!T

They speak for people who aren't around to attest to it. Even the dead.

They seldom keep their end of the bargain. If they do, their demeanor lets you know it's a burden, even if what you did for them was so they wouldn't be burdened by something.

Their favorite think to do is meddle.

Toxic people make their victims feel bad for things that they should feel bad for, instead of feeling bad.

CHICKENSH!T

When a friend asks them to do something, they say you are the reason they can't.

They are good about ignoring your calls but freak out if you don't answer after the first ring when calling you.

All play and no work, makes Jack unable to afford much.

Their friends are consoling them for the things that they did to you. Then when their friends tell them how awful you are to do that to them, they'll tell you what a jerk their friends think you are, without considering that had they told them the truth, their friends would think they're an awful jerk.

Its always a game to them.

They mess up their bed and leave it for others to make.

They will ask you to set an alarm for them to wake up, and if they sleep through it, it's your fault.

They hang-up the phone so that you talk until you realize they are no longer on the phone.

A chickenshit will let an innocent person take the blame for something they did and are too afraid to face themselves.

There is less time to fulfill your dreams if you are dealing with doo-doo.

CHICKENSH!T

They never remember their lies.

They will say,
"I'm not perfect!"
As if it takes perfection to not be abusive.

They will do something conniving right in front of you, knowing you are watching them, then deny they did it.

If you bought it, it now belongs to them.

CHICKENSH!T

You can offer a toxic person the most amazing cake, with perfect consistency, velvety frosting and delectable flavor, and they will disregard all its qualities to point out that a candle is crooked.

No matter how much you give them, they break your things when they get mad.

Using the term, "I am only human" for bad behavior is a copout. It suggests you know better but hold all humanity accountable for your choice to have it.

Their choices will pluck your life up if you let them.

Really! They are only pretending to have all the symptoms.

You could have toured the world 10 times over for all they know but share something you are doing on social media, and they will freak the phuck out!

The amount of anger they show when questioned on their behavior is training those that care to let them be stupid, come what may.

They consider using people a skill.

No! Making mistakes don't make you chickenshit. Blaming someone else for them while they pay the consequence, makes you a chickenshit. It also means that it wasn't a mistake.

They do not listen to care; they listen to take control.

CHICKENSH!T

If they lose something, they'll tear everything up, because nobody deserves anything if they can't find what they misplaced. And when they find it, they leave everything messed up.

If you are enjoying television and they want your attention, they might blast music and wait for you to say something so they can accuse you of trying to prevent them from enjoying themselves.

They behave like what they lost magically transported to the world of lost socks and guitar picks.

They beg to take you out to dinner, then have you pay for it.

CHICKENSH!T

They've called you every name in the book and the moment you decide to call them an a**hole, they will forever claim that you name call too.

Shut the phuck up already! Grow up! Heal! Go to therapy, AA or whatever you must do! Quit making a blithering idiot of yourself and making things harder for those that love you!

Subtle differences can change everything.

If they get hurt while throwing a tantrum, they'll say you did it.

"I DIDN'T DO ANYTHING!"

I say, I say, I say you did son!

There is a difference between doing something and denying it, and denying something that you didn't do.

If someone jumps to offer you help, they will intervene saying that they have no problem doing it, then they will never do it and you'll be too embarrassed to ask the person that offered.

A chickenshit is the first to suggest picking on someone, instead of including them.

They have a behavior most parents would admonish their child for.

CHICKENSH!T

They are using you as an excuse they can't keep obligations to other people.

"EVERYBODY BLAMES ME!"

Elementary my dear Watson!

Yelling over one another prevents communication.

Using the term, 'narcissist' as an insult, is so narcissistic.

CHICKENSH!T

After they convince their friends of a lie, then to them it becomes the truth.

How you take care of your belongings reflects how others will think you'd take care of them.

Stool is supposed to be for pidgeons!.

Getting you to do what they can be doing, is considered a feather in their cap.

They have a short fuse.

Hey you! Yeah, you! If a lot of what you have read applies to you, and you are still reading, then you must want to make a positive change. Coming this far says a lot. I am proud of you. I can only imagine how proud your loved ones will be. Ok, back to the poop scoop.

"THIS ALWAYS HAPPENS TO ME!"

You know darn well, what you need to do! . t, t, t, TODAY JUNIOR!

They say their sneaky association to people you know is always to see if they were going to do something bad to you, and not because they were doing something sneaky.

They lie a lot.

CHICKENSH!T

If the vice you use to relax, is the same thing that sets you off if you don't have it, might be an addiction.

It takes a chickenshit to pass the buck!

"Ignorance is bliss" until you've ran off the people that were dealing with your shit.

Their intensity keeps your nerves on edge, and the moment you lose your cool, the intense one, will be the first to say you need to calm down.

CHICKENSH!T

They deliberately huff & puff a way to get your attention while annoying you.

Don't drag your feet! If someone that drops everything to help you asks you a favor, there should be no hesitation.

Their trauma is what makes them so traumatizing.

5

Chicken Scratch
Food for Thought

Words are magic! Good or bad, they have the power to inflict pain and joy. How strong they are is dependent on the power we give them to harm or heal us.

You see, negative words and actions don't hurt us because we don't care, they hurt us because we do.

Whether it is because we would never want to hurt another person the way we are being hurt or because we are hurt over how thoughtless a person can be, or a double whammy, being hurt by someone we care for. What hurt them that now causes them to hurt us?

When we don't understand the magic of words, we build a shield out of the negative thing that has hurt us,

CHICKENSH!T

Thinking that if we stop feeling at all, then we can't be hurt. In turn we hurt ourselves more and can become just as harmful to others, thus what we don't like.

On the other hand, positive words are just as powerful, and it is up to us to decide what we want to give them the power to do.

Since we know that how we treat others can leave a lasting impression, do we want our words to have a negative effect that causes others to feel depressed, angry, and sad or do we want them to feel good, uplifted, and empowered? It is our choice.

It takes strength to counter the negative things that come at us. It's the kind of magic that says, you can't have my energy! Nothing defeats negativity better than positive energy.

CHICKENSH!T

Some people choose to fight fire with fire and fling their shit right back at those giving it to them and make even more of a mess.

Most of us avoid stepping in it.

All we can do is our best to understand and if they still want to exhaust us with a negative trip, we have the choice to waste our energy on it, or not put up with their shit.

Let them make mudpies for all you care! Use your magic and choose peace.

Shit be gone! POOF!

You don't need drama or theatrics to receive help. Kindly asking is much easier.

CHICKENSH!T

Manage your mood, or other people will.

Choose to heal.

Be helpful.

Don't stay cooped up!

Back in my day we had to, shape up or ship out!

Laugh, it's ok.

Choosing to heal is strength, choosing to be abusive is a choice,

There is a strength that can only be found in listening and when you find it, it becomes easy

Listening to someone with care, who wants to discuss how you have wronged them is a sign of maturity.

If you want to do something to someone for a reaction, do love, and do it on purpose.

If this book was a gift, someone's probably fed up. That can be changed.

CHICKENSH!T

LOVE YOURSELF!

Make it a point to smile at people you make eye contact with.

The cool people are not thinking about what makes them cool, they are busy focusing on their priorities, making awesome plans, and keeping their word, which is usually what makes them cool.

Always remember the Golden Rule.

CHICKENSH!T

They think you're beautiful and only you can change their mind. Quit trying to.

Shit or get off the pot!

Refusing to listen to reasonable advice prevents bullies from growing up.

When you're a child and you don't take care of your toys, they break, and you learn to take care of them, or you won't have them for long. This lesson applies to people as well.

Say you're sorry and truly mean it.

Your parents are no spring chickens, go easy on them.

Dream... find a goal, great or small, set out for adventure, go for it!

OMG! That thing you did that you wish you didn't do, that makes your heart sink every time you remember it! Forgive yourself! You have a conscience and you can't buy or put a price on it!

If they ask something simple of you, don't cop out. Just do it! You will feel good about yourself, and they will notice the effort.

If you're caught lying once, then it makes what you believe in look weak.

CHICKENSH!T

Mom & Pop,

If you are not a custodial parent that gets the child(ren) to doctor appointments, or meetings and band practice; to school and school-dances; buys school supplies, teen hygiene products, necessities, accessories, uniforms and the latest-styles; deals with emergencies, takes them on fieldtrips, and other extracurricular activity; provides allowance, finds child-care, is a taxi, drives to concerts, sleep-overs, sports/practice; cheers them on, coaches them, is a referee & umpire; is the one to discipline and be the bad guy; is a soundboard, consoles and cries with them; plans parties, makes sure they shower and eat; prepares meals, does the shopping; helps with homework, reading, nurturing; cuts hair, advocates for them, offers emotional support; does all of this while holding down a full-time job and loving every minute of it, while making sure they are ready to spend every other weekend with you; then may I suggest, instead of adding heartache to already full plate, by making disparaging comments or wondering where child support is going; that doesn't cover half of these expenses, that you make sure, that every single moment you have with our child is spent making amazing memories to cherish. Time is priceless. So is love and peace of mind.

CHICKENSH!T

You'll should never have to wonder why a friend isn't being friendly.

Conversation begins with talking,
Communication begins with listening.

Don't put effort into creating a bad mood. For you, or anybody else.

Take control of yourself, not others.

Good thoughts change the picture.

Don't be a name-calling potty mouth. A plunger is for a toilet, not your face.

It is easy to do nice things when you want to.
The challenge is doing them when you don't.

Try not talking so disrespectful to the people that love you. Stop making yourself out to be so ugly! They see you as the beautiful person that you are! Because you don't think that of yourself, you behave as if you aren't. Stop that!

Everybody makes mistakes. Everybody!

Don't become a negative Nellie.

CHICKENSH!T

I believe in you.
Believe in yourself.

Your opinion matters. It's important to remember it's not the only opinion that matters.

When you are ready to talk instead of yell you've reached a new plateau.

Rehab, AA, or therapy... I always found it fascinating how so many people have met the love of their life after taking this step.

CHICKENSH!T

Love & Sorry are actions words.

If someone says, "You're stupid for staying!" They have more in common with your abuser that they do you.

Imagine life without drama and be faithful to it.

Replace a bad attitude with gratitude.

If you think they avoid you like the plague, then maybe it's time to consider what it is about you that is toxic?

Phases are temporary.

Stop trying so hard to be a person you are not, when the easiest thing you can do, is to be you! Beautiful! Unique! Only one of you, YOU!

Settle somewhere you can grow wild. In a good way.

Find the courage to heal that terrible thing that happened to you in your past, so that you can stop being so mean-spirited and abusive to people who love you and who you're relying on to help you.

Once lying becomes a habit, the liar is usually the only one not aware of it.

CHICKENSH!T

A mother hen protects its chicks, cats, and puppies too.

Take your job seriously, but don't take it personally.

Get your hands dirty! Plant something and care for it.

Attend a live music gig.

CHICKENSH!T

A person in a good financial situation might tell you what they would do if they were in your situation, but rarely consider that if they were, then they wouldn't have their money to make it that easy. Keep going anyway!

Being insensitive to someone's hardship does not make you good at your job.
Being professional is a requirement, being cold-hearted is a choice.

Start a nest egg.

Remember that your abusive situation is not a training course.

Take your job seriously, but don't take it personally.

One day you will think about the people you love and be thankful you were able to experience life at the same time.

Whenever you catch yourself saying something negative, think of it as a comedy , and you will crack-up laughing.

Imagine spending your entire life trying to get a person to love you that made you feel unworthy of it.
Then don't ever do it.

Nobody will agree with you 100% of the time. Accept it!

No! It is not always Karma. Bad things happen to good people all the time.

CHICKENSH!T

The world is already full of too much unexpected drama, pain, and bullshit, to be in a relationship with a person that deliberately creates it,

"Birds of a Feather Flock together." Sometimes, it's better to fly solo.

Be who's best for you, not who's best for them.

Why are you more embarrassed to talk about your feelings than by your bad attitude?

CHICKENSH!T

Parents' guide us, but ultimately, we are responsible for our own choices.

If they get into trouble because they are a chip off the block, a heart-to-heart conversation is more effective than punishing them for the example you set.

Swearing to god, or on your kid's life, doesn't make a lie more credible, It makes a reasonable listener wonder why you think your lie it is so important to believe.

Use all that incredible energy to build yourself up instead sucking the life out of others.

When a word is used as an insult, its use is to hurt. When a word is used for its definition, it is to describe something, hence the name of this book.

Learn to bite your tongue.

Make it a point to smile at strangers that may need it.

Help to make common decency common again.

Don't play favorites. First come first served.

If someone says something bad about someone, be the one that finds something good to say, unless they are really that bad!

CHICKENSH!T

There are plenty of interesting things to talk about without making shit up!

When you feel bad that someone else is hurt, you know your heart is working.

Honor is everything.

Tell them you love them.

You don't have to fit into a mold.

CHICKENSH!T

A sincere apology speaks volumes for your character.

Forgive petty things quickly.

When a child becomes an adult, they still want their dad to think they are cool.

You're going to make a positive change this year. No if's and's or but's about it!

Make wonderful memories.

I hope good things happen for you.

Be someone that helps restore faith in humanity.

How you feel when you are around someone can let you know if you have a soul. It can also let you know if they have one.

Hug someone you love, for no reason.

Don't push your luck! It's not worth it.

Roosters share and talk sweetly to hens.

Like grandma always said, "It'll all come out in the wash!"

If they yell, ask if you can talk it out. It's worth a try.

CHICKENSH!T

Keep your promises.

Value small joys.

It's very hard to focus with chaos around you. If you must do this! This is a virtual hug. Keep going! You can do it!

You don't have to be together to work together.

CHICKENSH!T

Appreciation is another powerful magic!

Thinking twice about doing something that can have bad results, is a good habit.

Treasure the time you have here.

The word "failure" is mistaken for a derogatory term and applied to people that have at least tried. Keep trying!

CHICKENSH!T

Nowadays, too many people think that losing their cool, is cool. If you lose your cool, that's not cool. You've lost your cool! Now you are just a hot-head, full of hot-air and taking your steam out on cool people.

I suppose that is where the term, "chill out" was coined. So, chill! Don't blow your top or your bottom! Take a deep breath, It's all cool! Just try to keep it cool, without being cold. You know, cold-blooded. That's just mean! Balance is a good thing! Be cool!

Dick's been plucking for about ten years now.

Everything is a matter of circumstance.
People don't always see eye to eye.
Minds and opinions change over time.
That is the beauty of growing.
We love to watch it happen.
In flowers, trees, children, grandchildren, and ourselves.

GROWTH

Many times, we try to stop it.
We even invent things to try to prevent it,
and fight against it.
Like love,
It will always prevail.

CHICKENSH!T

The End

CHICKENSH!T

LOVE ONE ANOTHER

It's as simple as an ear to listen, a shoulder to cry on, or a hand to hold.

Dear Reader,

When our feelings are hurt, it tells us that our hearts are working. That's good! If we allow the hurt to consume us, then we are giving our energy to something that harms us. That's bad!

Energy is an invisible force, but it is very powerful! It is the force behind love, the sun, and what keeps everything alive. It's a gift for everyone and everything living. You can label it anyway you want, and you don't need to earn it, you just need to accept it.

When we put our energy into what brings us joy, we begin to rise above what is bringing us down. Figuratively speaking, heaven or hell? Joy lifts us up, anger brings us down. Be very careful what you give your energy to.

When positive thinking starts to do its magic, then you know that your faith is working!

There are a lot of things we can't see, and we know it's there because we feel it. And when you feel it, you'll begin to behave better and have an overall better outlook toward everything. People will notice, and they will want to know what happened.

Just like any instrument, all we need is a little fine tuning from time to time.

With love,
De Anna

Ideas

- ○ Discover the characteristics attributed to you.
- ○ Emphasize on your strengths.
- ○ Get ahead of responsibilities.
- ○ Bake something.
- ○ Try an ethnic food you've never had before.
- ○ Plant something and care for it.
- ○ Join a club, gym.
- ○ Visit an elderly friend or relative.
- ○ Donate old clothes.
- ✓ Read a book.
- ○ Spring-clean a room, no matter the season.
- ○ Find a hobby; sew, crafts, sculpting.
- ○ Go for walks.
- ○ Start a puzzle.
- ○ Listen to good mood music.
- ○ Join that adult softball team!
- ○ Chat with the birds.
- ○ Hatch a fun plan.
- ○ Fly a kite.
- ○ Ride a bike.
- ○ Tell your family you love them.
- ○ Smile often and for no reason.

CHICKENSH!T

THE BROOD

The Word Birds

Tom   Frazz

Dick   Blabs

Harry   Henna

CHICKENSH!T

RESOURCES 📱

988 is the new **National Mental Health Hotline.**

SAMSA **Substance Abuse and Mental Health Services Hotline.**
1-800-662-HELP (4357)

The **National Domestic Violence Hotline** (NDVH) is a 24-hour confidential service.
1-800-799-SAFE (7233)

Emotional and Domestic Abuse
CRISIS TEXT LINE free 24/7 support.
Text : 741741

Al-Anon Family Groups
https://al-anon.org

Alcoholics Anonymous
https://www.aa.org/find-aa

www.ingramcontent.com/pod-product-compliance
Lightning Source LLC
Chambersburg PA
CBHW061657040426
42446CB00010B/1780